introduction

Cowls are one of my favorite garments to crochet. I love how they add just a touch of warmth on days when the weather is changing—perfect for evenings in the fall and spring, and always useful when going from indoors to out, even in the summer. I always have one near at hand for whatever situation arises.

They're also just fun to make. You can finish one in just a few hours, and even use it as an opportunity to learn a new stitch pattern. Because they take so little time and yarn, they make perfect gifts for any occasion!

The twelve patterns in this book are all unique, offering something for everyone. Get your hooks out and start stitching today!

contents

17

20

22

24

26

29

sweet and sour cowl

up a loop] three times, yarn over and draw through all 4 loops on hook.

Yarn

Astra by Patons, 1¾oz/50g skeins, each approx 161yd/147m (acrylic)

- 1 skein each in Navy #02849, Emerald #02708, Purple #02740 and Oz #08200 or any number of colors you like

Hook

Size G/6 (4mm) crochet hook OR SIZE NEEDED TO OBTAIN GAUGE

Finished Measurements

7½"/19cm tall x 24"/61cm wide at bottom hem, 21"/53 wide at top hem

Gauge

Finished motif is approximately 1½"/4cm square.
TAKE TIME TO CHECK YOUR GAUGE.

Note

Ch-3 counts as 1 dc throughout.

Special Stitches

sc2tog (single crochet 2 sts together) [Insert hook in next st, yarn over and draw up a loop] twice, yarn over and draw through all 3 loops on hook.

sc3tog (single crochet 3 sts together) [Insert hook in next st, yarn over and draw

Cowl

Row 1: First Square

With any color, ch 3, join into ring with sl st in first ch.

Rnd 1 Ch 3, 2 dc in ring, (ch 3, 3 dc in ring) 3 times, ch 3, join rnd with sl st in top of beg-ch. End off—12 dc/4 3-dc shells.

Row 1: Squares 2–5

With any color, ch 3, join into ring with sl st in first ch.

Rnd 1 Ch 3, 2 dc in ring, (ch 3, 3 dc in ring) 2 times, ch 1, sl st in adjacent ch-3 sp of previous motif, ch 1, 3 dc in ring, ch 1, sl st in adjacent ch-3 sp of previous motif, ch 1, join rnd with sl st in top of beg-ch. End off.

Row 2: Square 1

Ch 3, 2 dc in ring, (ch 3, 3 dc in ring) 2 times, ch 1, sl st in adjacent ch-3 sp of Square 1 of prev row, ch 1, 3 dc in ring, ch 1, sl st in ch-3 sp of motif diagonally across, ch 1, join rnd with sl st in top of beg-ch. End off.

Row 2: Squares 2–4

With any color, ch 3, join into ring with sl st in first ch.

Rnd 1 Ch 3, 2 dc in ring, ch 3, 3 dc in ring, ch 1, sl st in adjacent ch-3 sp of previous motif, ch 1, (3 dc in ring, ch 1, sl st in ch-3

sp of motif diagonally across, ch 1) 2 times, join rnd with sl st in top of beg-ch. End off.

Row 2: Square 5

With any color, ch 3, join rnd with sl st in first ch.

Rnd 1 Ch 3, 2 dc in ring, ch 3, 3 dc in ring, ch 1, sl st in adjacent ch-3 sp of previous motif, ch 1, 3 dc in ring, ch 1, sl st in adjacent ch-3 sp of motif diagonally across, ch 1, 3 dc in ring, ch 1, sl st in adjacent ch-3 sp of motif below, ch 1, join rnd with sl st in top of beg-ch. End off.

Rows 3–14

Rep Row 2.

Add two additional squares on either side of front opening using instructions for Row 1 Square 2 and Row 2 Square 2.

Finishing

Edging

Rnd 1 With RS facing and any color, starting in any st, sc around entire work placing 1 sc in each dc and ch-1 sp around, 3 sc in each corner and sc2tog in each valley at the top of the 2-motif column at front opening. Join rnd with sl st in first sc, ch 1, do not turn.

Rnd 2 With same color, sc in each sc around, placing 3 sc in each corner and working an sc3tog over each sc2tog plus the sc on either side. End off. Weave in ends.

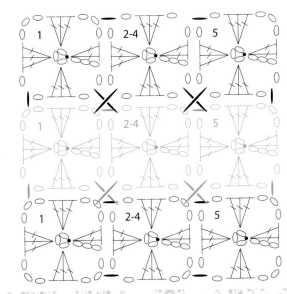

- • Slip stitch (sl st)
- | Sl st into adjacent ch-sp
- ✕ Sl st into ch-sp diagonally across
- ◯ Chain (ch)
- ⊤ Double crochet (dc)

cotton candy cowl

Yarn 5

Bamboo Natural Blends by Bernat, 2.10oz/60g skeins, each approx 63yd/57m (bamboo/acrylic/polyester)

- 4 skeins each in Lotus #92420 (A) and Almond Blossom #92426 (B)

Hook

Size K/10½ (6.5mm) crochet hook OR SIZE NEEDED TO OBTAIN GAUGE

Additional

Tapestry needle

Finished Measurements

8"/20cm x 68"/172cm

Gauge

12 sts and 14 rows to 4"/10cm over pattern stitch.
TAKE TIME TO CHECK YOUR GAUGE.

Cowl

With A, ch 25.

Row 1 Sc in 2nd ch from hook and in each ch across—24 sc. Ch 1, turn.

Row 2 Sc through back loops only in each sc across. Ch 1, turn.

Rep Row 2 for pattern until work measures 34"/86cm from start.

Change to B, rep row 2 for pattern until work measures 68"/172cm from start. End off.

Finishing

Form cowl into a ring without twisting; sew seam with tapestry needle.

Edging

Work 1 rnd sc evenly across each long side, using A when working across A rows and B when working across B rows. Join each rnd with sl st in first sc.

Weave in ends.

denim cowl

Yarn

Sugar'n Cream Denim by Lily, 2½oz/71g skeins, each approx 120yd/109m (cotton)
• 3 skeins in Blue Jeans #01116

Hook

Size H/8 (5mm) crochet hook OR SIZE NEEDED TO OBTAIN GAUGE

Additional

7½"/1cm shank buttons
Tapestry needle

Finished Measurements

6"/15cm tall by 40"/102cm wide, unbuttoned

Gauge

13 sts and 10 rows to 4"/10 cm over pattern stitch.
TAKE TIME TO CHECK YOUR GAUGE.

Note

Ch-3 counts as 1 dc throughout.

Special Stitches

puff stitch (puff st) Yo, insert hook in next st, yo, draw through st, (yo, insert hook in same st, yo, draw through st) 4 times, yo draw through 10 loops on hook, yo, draw through 2 loops on hook.

Cowl

Ch 126.
Row 1 Sc in back or bump of 2nd ch from hook and in back or bump of each ch across—125 sc. Ch 3, turn.
Row 2 Puff st in first sc, *ch 1, sk 1 sc, puff st in next sc; rep from * to end, dc in last sc—62 puff sts + 2 dc. Ch 1, turn.
Row 3 Sc in first dc, sc in next puff st, *sc in next ch-1 sp, sc in next puff st; rep from * to end, sc in last dc—125 sc. Ch 3, turn.
Row 4 Dc in next sc, puff st in next sc, *ch 1, sk 1 sc, puff st in next sc; rep from * across until 2 sc remain, dc in each of last 2 sc—61 puff sts + 4 dc. Ch 1, turn.
Row 5 Sc in each of first 2 dc, sc in next puff st, *sc in next ch-1 sp, sc in next puff st; rep from * across until 2 dc remain, sc in each of last 2 dc—125 sc. Ch 3, turn.
Rows 6–15 Rep Rows 2–5 twice, then Rows 2–4 once more. Fasten off after Row 15.

Finishing

Work 1 rnd sc around entire piece, working 3 sc in each corner so it lies flat. Join rnd with sl st in first sc. Sew buttons to RS of one short end, and use sps between 1st dc and 1st puff st on each row of opposite end as button holes.

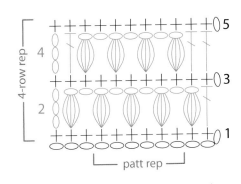

SYMBOL KEY

⬭ ch

+ sc

⊤ dc

⬭ puff st

pumpkin spice cowl

Yarn 5

Wool-Ease Chunky by Lion Brand Yarn, 5 oz/140g skeins, each approx 153yd/140m (acrylic/wool)

• 2 skeins in Pumpkin #630-133 (A)

Homespun by Lion Brand Yarn, 6oz/170g skeins, each approx 185yd/169m (acrylic/polyester)

• 1 skein in Deco #790-309 (B)

Hook

Size L/11 (8mm) crochet hook OR SIZE NEEDED TO OBTAIN GAUGE

Additional

Tapestry needle

Finished Measurements

16"/41cm x 26"/66cm measured in center of row

Gauge

12 sts/4 3-sc shells and 9 rows to 4"/10cm over hdc.
TAKE TIME TO CHECK YOUR GAUGE.

Note

Ch-2 counts as 1 hdc.

Cowl

Ch 41.

Row 1 3 sc in 2nd ch from hook, *sk 2 ch, 3 sc in next ch; rep from * to end—42 sc/14 3-sc shells. Ch 1, turn.

Row 2 Sk 1 sc, 3 sc in next sc, *sk 2 sts, 3 sc in next sc; rep from * to end. Ch 1, turn.

Row 3 Sk 1 sc, 3 sc in next sc, *sk 2 sts, 3 sc in next sc; rep from * 3 more times, sk 1 sc, sl st in next sc—15 sc/5 3-sc shells. Ch 1, turn.

Row 4 Rep Row 2.

Row 5 Rep Row 2 all the way across work—42 sc/14 3-sc shells

Rows 6–8 Rep Rows 3–5.

Rows 9–11 Rep Row 2.

Rep Rows 3–11 nine times, then Rows 3–10 once. End off.

Finishing

Whip stitch the seam together—the finished piece will have an hourglass shape.

Edging

Rnd 1 With B work 1 rnd sc evenly spaced around neck opening of cowl. Join rnd with sl st in first sc.

Rnd 2 Ch 2, hdc in each sc around. Join rnd with sl st in top of beg-ch.

Rnd 3 Ch 1, sc in same st as sl st and in each hdc around. Join rnd with sl st in first sc. End off.

Turn work inside out so the opposite side of the other opening is facing you, and repeat edging instructions.

Weave in all ends.

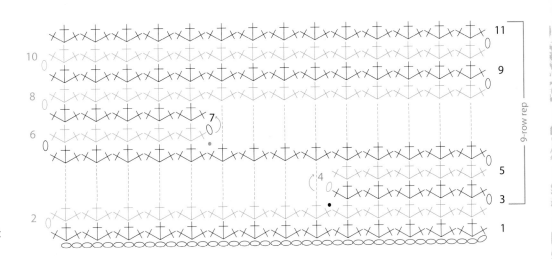

• sl st
◦ ch
⨯†⨯ 3 sc in same st

tutti frutti

Yarn
Amazing by Lion Brand Yarn.
1¾oz/50g skeins, each approx
147yd/135m (wool/acrylic)
• 3 skeins in Aurora #825-200

Hook
Size J/10 (6.0mm) crochet hook
OR SIZE NEEDED TO OBTAIN
GAUGE

Finished Measurements
16"/41cm x 44"/112cm in diameter

Gauge
12 sts and 8 rnds to 4"/10cm over pattern st.
TAKE TIME TO CHECK YOUR GAUGE.

Note
Ch-3 counts as 1 dc throughout.

Cowl
First Half
Ch 132. Join into a ring with sc in back or
bump of first ch, being careful not to twist sts.
Rnd 1 Ch 1, sc in back or bump of each ch
around. Join rnd with sl st in first ch—132 sc.
Rnd 2 Ch 3, 2 dc in same sc as sl st, sk 2 sc, sc
in next sc, *sk 2 sc, 5 dc in next sc, sk 2 sc, sc
in next sc; rep from * around, ending with sk 2
sc, 2 dc in same st as first 3 dc. Join rnd with sl
st in top of beg-ch—22 5-dc shells.
Rnd 3 Ch 1, sc in same ch as sl st, sk 2 dc, 5 dc
in next sc, *sk 2 dc, sc in next dc, sk 2 dc, 5 dc
in next sc; rep from * around, ending with sk 2
dc, join rnd with sl st in first sc.
Rnd 4 Ch 3, 2 dc in same sc as sl st, sk 2 dc, sc
in next dc, * sk 2 dc, 5 dc in next sc, sk 2 dc, sc
in next dc; rep from * around, ending with sk 2
dc, 2 dc in same sc as first 3 dc. Join rnd with sl
st in top of beg ch.
Rep Rnds 3 & 4 until work measures 8"/20cm or
half of desired total width from foundation ch.

Second Half
Join yarn with sl st in opposite side of foundation ch in base of any 5-dc shell. Rep instructions for First Half beginning with Rnd 2.

Finishing
Weave in all ends. Block lightly if desired.

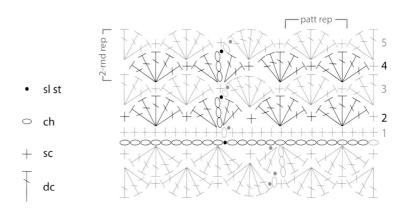

• sl st
○ ch
+ sc
⊤ dc

citrus mobius

Yarn 〔3〕

Baby Soft by Lion Brand Yarn,
5oz/140g skeins, each approx
459yd/420m (acrylic/nylon)
• 1 skein in Lavender #920-143

Hooks

Size G/6 (4mm) crochet hook
OR SIZE NEEDED TO OBTAIN
GAUGE

Finished Measurements

11"/28cm x 44"/112cm

Gauge

18 sts/1 pattern repeat and 8 rows measures 4"/10cm over pattern st.
TAKE TIME TO CHECK YOUR GAUGE.

Notes

Ch-3 counts as 1 dc.
Ch-4 counts as 1 dc + 1 ch.

Cowl

Ch 199 loosely.
Row 1 Sc in the back or bump of 2nd ch
from hook and in back or bump of each ch
across—198 sc.
Join into round with a sc in first ch of row,
being careful to twist the work 180 degrees.
In other words, the first sc of Rnd 1 will be
in the opposite side of the foundation ch
from the first sc of Row 1.
Rnd 1 Joining sc counts as first sc, *ch 3,
sk 3 ch, sc in next ch, sk 4 ch, 9 dc in next
ch, sk 4 ch, sc in next ch, ch 3, sk 3 ch, sc in
next ch; rep from * around, switching from
the bottom of Row 1 to the top of Row 1
when you come to the Row 1 join, and re-
placing final sc with a sl st in first sc to join
rnd—22 9-dc shells for base of pineapples
& 44 ch-3 sps.
Rnd 2 Ch 4, 2 dc in same sc as sl st, *ch
1, sk ch-3 sp and sc, [dc in next dc, ch 1] 9
times, sk sc and ch-3 sp, (2 dc, ch 1, 2 dc) in
next sc; rep from * 20 times more, ch 1, sk
ch-3 sp and sc, [dc in next dc, ch 1] 9 times,
sk sc and ch-3 sp, dc in first sc, join rnd with
sl st in top of beg-ch.
Rnd 3 Sl st in first ch-1 sp, ch 4, 2 dc in
same ch-1 sp, *ch 3, sk ch-1 sp, sc in next
ch-1 sp, [ch 3, sc in next ch-1 sp] 7 times, ch
3, sk ch-1 sp, (2 dc, ch 1, 2 dc) in next ch-1
sp; rep from * 20 times more, ch 3, sk ch-1
sp, sc in next ch-1 sp, [ch 3, sc in next ch-1
sp] 7 times, ch 3, sk ch-1 sp, dc in first ch-1
sp, join rnd with sl st in top of beg-ch.
Rnd 4 Sl st in first ch-1 sp, ch 4, 2 dc in
same ch-1 sp, *ch 3, sk ch-3 sp, sc in next
ch-3 sp, [ch 3, sc in next ch-3 sp] 6 times, ch

SYMBOL KEY

• sl st
◦ ch
+ sc
† dc

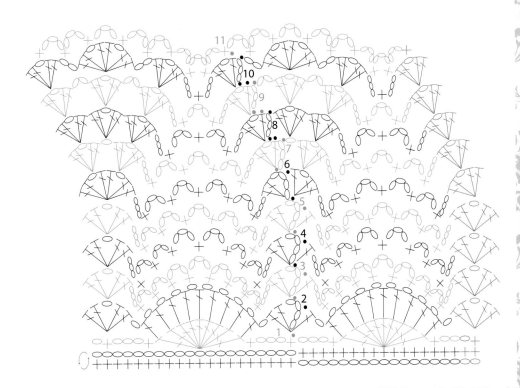

15

citrus mobius

3, sk ch-3 sp, (2 dc, ch 1, 2 dc) in next ch-1 sp. Rep from *
20 times more, ch 3, sk ch-3 sp, sc in next ch-3 sp, [ch 3, sc
in next ch-3 sp] 6 times, ch 3, sk ch-3 sp, dc in first ch-1 sp,
join rnd with sl st in top of beg-ch.

Rnd 5 Rep Rnd 4, working bracketed [ ] directions only 5
times.

Rnd 6 Sl st in first ch-1 sp, ch 4, 2 dc in same ch-1 sp, *ch
3, sk ch-3 sp, sc in next ch-3 sp, [ch 3, sc in next ch-3 sp]
4 times, ch 3, sk ch-3 sp, (2 dc, ch 1, 2 dc, ch 1, 2 dc) in
next ch-1 sp. Rep from * 20 times more, ch 3, sk ch-3 sp, sc
in next ch-3 sp, [ch 3, sc in next ch-3 sp] 4 times, ch 3, sk
ch-3 sp, (2 dc, ch 1, dc) in first ch-1 sp, join rnd with sl st in
top of beg-ch.

Rnd 7 Sl st in first ch-1 sp, ch 3, (dc, ch 1, 2 dc) in same
ch-1 sp, *ch 3, sk ch-3 sp, sc in next ch-3 sp, [ch 3, sc in
next ch-3 sp] 3 times, ch 3, sk ch-3 sp, (2 dc, ch 1, 2 dc)
in next ch-1 sp, ch 1, (2 dc, ch 1, 2 dc) in next ch-1 sp; rep
from * 20 times more. Ch 3, sk ch-3 sp, sc in next ch-1 sp,
(ch 3, sc in next ch-1 sp) 3 times, ch 3, sk ch-3 sp, (2 dc, ch
1, 2 dc) in ch-1 sp, ch 1, join rnd with sl st in top of beg-ch.

Rnd 8 Sl st in next dc and in first ch-1 sp, ch 3, (dc, ch 1,
2 dc) in same ch-1 sp, *ch 3, sk ch-3 sp, sc in next ch-3 sp,
[ch 3, sc in next ch-3 sp] 2 times, ch 3, sk ch-3 sp, (2 dc, ch
1, 2 dc in next ch-1 sp) 3 times; rep from * 20 times more,
ch 3, sk ch-3 sp, sc in next ch-3 sp, [ch 3, sc in next ch-3
sp] 2 times, ch 3, sk ch-3 sp, (2 dc, ch 1, 2 dc) in each of
next 2 ch-1 sps, join rnd with sl st in top of beg-ch.

Rnd 9 Sl st in next dc and in first ch-1 sp, ch 3, (dc, ch 1,
2 dc) in same ch-1 sp, *ch 3, sk ch-3 sp, sc in next ch-3 sp,
ch 3, sc in next ch-3 sp, ch 3, sk ch-3 sp, [(2 dc, ch 1, 2 dc)
in next ch-1 sp, ch 2] 2 times, (2 dc, ch 1, 2dc) in next ch-1
sp; rep from * 20 times more, ch 3, sk ch-3 sp, sc in next
ch-3 sp, ch 3, sc in next ch-3 sp, ch 3, sk ch-3 sp, [(2 dc, ch
1, 2 dc) in next ch-1 sp, ch 2] twice, join rnd with sl st in
top of beg-ch.

Rnd 10 Sl st in next dc and in first ch-1 sp, ch 3, (dc, ch
1, 2 dc) in same ch-1 sp, *ch 3, sk ch-3 sp, sc in next ch-3
sp, ch 3, sk ch-3 sp, (2 dc, ch 1, 2 dc) in next ch-1 sp, ch 2,
sk ch-2 sp, (2 dc, ch 1, 2dc, ch 1, 2 dc) in next ch 1, sp, ch
2, sk ch-2 sp, (2 dc, ch 1, 2 dc) in next ch-1 sp; rep from *
20 times more, ch 3, sk ch-3 sp, sc in next ch-3 sp, ch 3, sk
ch-3 sp, (2 dc, ch 1, 2 dc) in next ch-1 sp, ch 2, sk ch-2 sp,
(2 dc, ch 1, 2 dc, ch 1, 2 dc) in next ch-1 sp, ch 2, join rnd
with sl st in top of beg-ch.

Rnd 11 Sl st in next dc, sc in first ch-1 sp, *ch 3, sc in next
ch-sp; rep from * around, working scs in each ch-1, ch-2,
and ch-3 sp, join rnd with sl st in first sc. End off.

Finishing
Weave in ends. Block lightly if desired.

lady apple

Yarn 4
Boutique Treasure by Red Heart, 3½oz/100g skeins, each approx 151yd/138m (acrylic/wool)
• 4 skeins in Abstract #1918

Hooks
Size N/15 (10mm), M/13 (9mm), L/11 (8mm), K/10½ (6.5mm), J/10 (6mm), I/9 (5.5mm), and H/8 (5mm) crochet hooks

Additional
6 buttons, 1"/2.5cm diameter
Tapestry needle

Finished Measurements
18"/46cm tall x 48"/122cm wide at bottom, 21"/53cm wide at top exclusive of button bands

Gauge
7 sts and 6 rows to 4"/10cm over pattern st. GAUGE IS NOT CRITICAL FOR THIS PROJECT.

Note
Ch-2 does not count as a st throughout.

Special Stitches
Pf (puff stitch) (yo, insert hook in st, yo, draw through st) 3 times, yo, draw through 6 loops on hook, yo, draw through 2 loops on hook.
Pf2tog (two puff sts together) [(yo, insert hook in designated st, yo, draw through st) 3 times] twice, yo, draw through 12 loops on hook, yo, draw through 2 loops on hook.

Cowl
With N/15 (10mm) hook, ch 128.
Row 1 3 sc in 2nd ch from hook, sc in each of next 9 ch, *sk 2 ch, sc in each of next 9 ch, 5 sc in next ch, sc in each of next 9 ch; rep from * 4 more times, sk 2 ch, sc in each of next 9 ch, 3 sc in last ch—6 points. Ch 1, turn.
Row 2 (RS) 2 sc in first sc, sc in each of next 10 sc, *sk 2 sc, sc in each of next 10 sc, 3 sc in next sc, sc in each of next 10 sc; rep from * 4 more times, sk 2 sc, sc in each of next 10 sc, 3 sc in last sc. Ch 1, turn.
Row 3 Rep Row 2, ch 2, turn.
Row 4 Pf in first sc, (ch 1, sk 1 sc, pf in next sc) 4 times, *ch 1, sk 1 sc, pf2tog beginning in next sc, sk 2 sc, finish pf2tog in next sc, (ch 1, sk 1 sc, pf in next sc) 9 times; rep

from * 4 more times, ch 1, sk 1 sc, pf2tog beginning in next sc, sk 2 sc, finish pf2tog in next sc, (ch 1, sk 1 sc, pf in next sc) 5 times—60 pf sts including pf2togs as 1 each. Ch 1, turn.
Row 5 Change to next smallest hook, 3 sc in first pf, *(sc in next ch-1 sp, sc in next pf) 4 times, sc in next ch-1 sp, sk pf2tog, sc in next ch-1 sp, (sc in next pf, sc in next ch-1 sp) 4 times, 5 sc in next pf. Rep from * 5 times, placing only 3 sc in last pf. Ch 1, turn.
Rows 6 & 7 Rep Rows 2 & 3.
Rows 8–21 Rep Rows 4–7 three more times then Rows 4 & 5 once more.
Row 22 2 sc in first sc, sc in each of next 8 sc, sc2tog, *sk 2 sc, sc2tog, sc in each of next 8 sc, 3 sc in next sc, sc in each of next 8 sc, sc2tog; rep from * 4 more times, sk 2 sc, sc2tog, sc in each of next 8 sc, 3 sc in last sc. Ch 1, turn.
Row 23 2 sc in first sc, sc in each of next 7 sc, sc2tog, *sk 2 sc, sc2tog, sc in each of next 7 sc, 3 sc in next sc, sc in each of next 7 sc, sc2tog; rep from * 4 more times, sk 2

lady apple

sc, sc in each of next 7 sc, 3 sc in last sc. Ch 1, turn.

Row 24 Pf in first sc, (ch 1, sk 1 sc, pf in next sc) 3 times, *ch 1, sk 1 sc, pf2tog beginning in next sc, sk 2 sc, finish pf2tog in next sc, (ch 1, sk 1 sc, pf in next sc) 7 times; rep from * 4 more times, ch 1, sk 1 sc, pf2tog beginning in next sc, sk 2 sc, finish pf2tog in next sc, (ch 1, sk 1 sc, pf in next sc) 4 times—48 pf sts including pf2togs. Ch 1, turn.

Row 25 Change to next smallest hook, 3 sc in first pf, *(sc in next ch-1 sp, sc in next pf) 3 times, sc in next ch-1 sp, sk pf2tog, sc in next ch-1 sp, (sc in next pf, sc in next ch-1 sp) 3 times, 5 sc in next pf. Rep from * 5 times, placing only 3 sc in last pf. Ch 1, turn.

Row 26 2 sc in first sc, sc in each of next 6 sc, sc2tog, *sk 2 sc, sc2tog, sc in each of next 6 sc, 3 sc in next sc, sc in each of next 6 sc, sc2tog; rep from * 4 more times, sk 2 sc, sc2tog, sc in each of next 6 sc, 3 sc in last sc. Ch 1, turn.

Row 27 2 sc in first sc, sc in each of next 5 sc, sc2tog, *sk 2 sc, sc2tog, sc in each of next 5 sc, 3 sc in next sc, sc in each of next 5 sc, sc2tog; rep from * 4 more times, sk 2 sc, sc in each of next 5 sc, 3 sc in last sc. Ch 1, turn.

Row 28 Pf in first sc, (ch 1, sk 1 sc, pf in next sc) 2 times, *ch 1, sk 1 sc, pf2tog beginning in next sc, sk 2 sc, finish pf2tog in next sc, (ch 1, sk 1 sc, pf in next sc) 5 times; rep from * 4 more times, ch 1, sk 1 sc, pf2tog beginning in next sc, sk 2 sc, finish

pf2tog in next sc, (ch 1, sk 1 sc, pf in next sc) 3 times—36 pf sts including pf2togs. Ch 1, turn.

Row 29 Change to next smallest hook, 3 sc in first pf, *(sc in next ch-1 sp, sc in next pf) 2 times, sc in next ch-1 sp, sk pf2tog, sc in next ch-1 sp, (sc in next pf, sc in next ch-1 sp) 2 times, 5 sc in next pf; rep from * 5 times, placing only 3 sc in last pf. Ch 1, turn.

Row 30 2 sc in first sc, sc in each of next 4 sc, sc2tog, *sk 2 sc, sc2tog, sc in each of next 4 sc, 3 sc in next sc, sc in each of next 4 sc, sc2tog; rep from * 4 more times, sk 2 sc, sc2tog, sc in each of next 4 sc, 3 sc in last sc. Ch 1, turn.

Row 31 2 sc in first sc, sc in each of next 3 sc, sc2tog, *sk 2 sc, sc2tog, sc in each of next 5 sc, 3 sc in next sc, sc in each of next 3 sc, sc2tog; rep from * 4 more times, sk 2 sc, sc in each of next 3sc, 3 sc in last sc. End off.

Finishing
Button Band
Row 1 With RS facing and K/10½ (6.5mm) hook, work 40 sc evenly spaced along left front edge. Ch 1, turn.
Row 2 Sc in each sc across. Ch 3, turn.
Row 3 Dc in each sc across. Ch 1, turn.
Row 4 Sc in each dc across. Ch 1, turn.
Row 5 Sc in each dc across. End off.

Buttonhole Band
Row 1 With RS facing and K/10½ (6.5mm) hook, work 40 sc evenly spaced along right

front edge. Ch 1, turn.
Row 2 Sc in each sc across. Ch 3, turn.
Row 3 Dc in next sc, *ch 1, sk 1 sc, dc in each of next 6 sts; rep from * 4 times, ch 1, sk 1 dc, dc in each of last 2 sc. Ch 1, turn.
Row 4 Sc in each dc and ch-1 sp across. Ch 1, turn.
Row 5 Sc in each sc across. End off.

Weave in all ends. Block very lightly if desired.

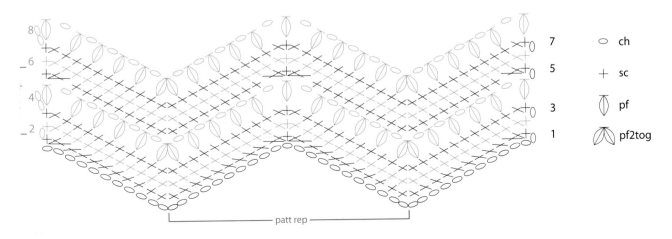

◯	ch
+	sc
〵	pf
〳	pf2tog

patt rep

pull-through scarf

Yarn 4
With Love by Coats and Clark,
6.98oz/198g skeins, each
approx 390yd/357 m (acrylic)
• 2 skeins True Blue #1814 (A),
  1 skein Cornsilk #1207 (B)

Hook
Size K/10½ (6.5mm) crochet
hook OR SIZE NEEDED TO
OBTAIN GAUGE

Additional
Tapestry needle

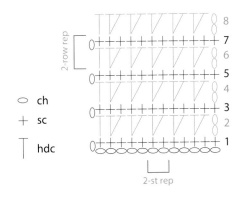

Finished Measurements
8"/20cm x 44"/112cm assembled.

Gauge
12 sts and 10 rows measures 4"/10 cm over
pattern stitch.
TAKE TIME TO CHECK YOUR GAUGE.

Note
Ch-2 counts as 1 hdc throughout.

Cowl
With A ch 25.
Row 1 (WS) Sc in 2nd ch from hook and in
each ch across—24 sc.
Row 2 2 hdc in 2nd sc, *sk 1 sc, 2 hdc in
next sc; rep from * across, ending with hdc
in last sc—24 hdc. Ch 1, turn.
Row 3 Sc in each hdc across—24 sc. Ch 2,
turn.
Rep Rows 2 & 3 for pattern until work
measures 8½"/21cm from start, ending with
a Row 3.
Turning Row (RS) Rep Row 2, working in
back loop only of each sc used.
Continue on in pattern as established
(rep Rows 2 & 3) until work measures

45"/114cm from start (36½"/93cm from
turning row), ending with a Row 3.

Ruffle
Row 1 2 hdc in 2nd sc, 2 hdc in each sc
across to last sc, hdc in last sc—46 hdc. Ch
1, turn.
Row 2 Sc in each hdc across. Ch 2, turn.
Rows 3 & 4 Rep Rows 1 & 2—90 sts.
Rep Rows 2 & 3 of Cowl until work measures 7½"/19cm from start of Ruffle, ending
with a Row 3. End off.

Finishing
Fold bottom of cowl to the WS at the turning row to form a wide casing; stitch into
place with tapestry needle and A.

Edging
Rnd 1 With A, beginning in any st, work
1 rnd sc all the way around the assembled
cowl, using the open front loops when you
come to the fold line, and placing 3 sc in
each corner so the work lays flat. Join rnd
with sl st in first sc; end off A.
Rnd 2 With B, beginning in any st, sc in
each sc around, placing 3 sc in each corner.
Join rnd with sl st in first sc. End off.
Weave in ends.

blue raspberry cowl

Yarn (5)

Serenity Chunky Weight by Premier Yarns, 3½oz/100g skeins, each approx 109yd/100m (acrylic)

- 2 skeins in Bonnie Blue #DN700-28

Hook

Size L/11 (8.0mm) crochet hook OR SIZE NEEDED TO OBTAIN GAUGE

Additional

3 buttons, 1¼"/3cm diameter
Tapestry needle

Finished Measurements

11"/28cm x 28"/71cm unbuttoned

Gauge

8 sts and 6 rows to 4"/10cm over cable pattern.
TAKE TIME TO CHECK YOUR GAUGE.

Note

Ch-2 counts as 1 hdc throughout.

Special Stitches

Left Twist (LT) Sk 1 bpdc, fpdc in next bpdc, reaching in front of st just worked, fpdc in skipped bpdc.

Left Cable (LC) Sk 1 bpdc, fpdc in each of next 2 bpdc, reaching in front of st just worked, fpdc in skipped bpdc.

Cowl

Ch 57.

Row 1 (WS) Hdc in 3rd ch from hook and in each ch across—56 hdc. Ch 2, turn.

Row 2 (RS) Hdc in each of next 4 hdc (5 hdc made, counting ch-2 as 1 hdc), fpdc in each of next 2 hdc, *hdc in each of next 2 hdc, fpdc in each of next 3 hdc, hdc in each of next 2 hdc, fpdc in each of next 2 hdc; rep from * 4 more times, hdc in each of last 4 hdc—27 fpdc, 29 htc. Ch 2, turn.

Row 3 Hdc in each of next 3 hdc, bpdc in each of next 2 fpdc, *hdc in each of next 2 hdc, bpdc in each of next 3 fpdc, hdc in each of next 2 hdc, bpdc in each of next 2 fpdc; rep from * 4 more times, hdc in each of next 2 hdc, ch 1, sk 1 hdc, hdc in each of last 2 hdc—27 bpdc, 28 htc, 1 ch-sp. Ch 2, turn.

Row 4 Hdc in next hdc, hdc in ch-1 sp, hdc in each of next 2 hdc, LT, *hdc in each of next 2 hdc, LC, hdc in each of next 2 hdc, LT; rep from * 4 more times, hdc in each of last 4 hdc. Ch 2, turn.

Row 5 Hdc in each of next 3 dc, bpdc in each of next 2 fpdc, *hdc in each of next 2 hdc, bpdc in each of next 3 fpdc, hdc in each of next 2 hdc, bpdc in each of next 2 fpdc; rep from * 4 more times, hdc in each of last 5 hdc. Ch 2, turn.

Row 6 Hdc in each of next 4 hdc, LT, *hdc in each of next 2 hdc, LC, hdc in each of next 2 hdc, LT; rep from * 4 more times, hdc in each of last 4 hdc. Ch 2, turn.

Row 7 Rep Row 5.

Row 8 Hdc in next hdc, ch 1, sk 1 hdc, hdc in each of next 2 hdc, LT, *hdc in each of next 2 hdc, LC, hdc in each of next 2 hdc, LT; rep from * 4 more times, hdc in each of last 4 hdc. Ch 2, turn.

Row 9 Hdc in each of next 3 dc, bpdc in each of next 2 fpdc, *hdc in each of next 2 hdc, bpdc in each of next 3 fpdc, hdc in each of next 2 hdc, bpdc in each of next 2 fpdc; rep from * 4 more times, hdc in next hdc, hdc in ch-1 sp, hdc in each of next 2 hdc. Ch 2, turn.

Row 10 Rep Row 6.

Row 11 Rep Row 5.

Row 12 Rep Row 6.

Row 13 Rep Row 3.

Row 14 Rep Row 4.

Row 15 Rep Row 5.

Row 16 Hdc in each st across. End off.

Finishing

Weave in ends.

With RS facing, work 1 rnd sc from left to right around cowl, making sure to work 3 sts in each corner so the work lays flat.

Sew buttons in place opposite buttonholes.

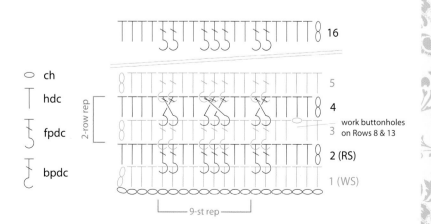

ch
hdc
fpdc
bpdc

2-row rep

16
5
4
3 — work buttonholes on Rows 8 & 13
2 (RS)
1 (WS)

9-st rep

pomegranate cowl

Yarn ②

Serenity Garden by Premier Yarns. 2oz/65g skeins, each approx 185yd/169m (microfiber)
• 3 skeins in Hibiscus #800-03

Hooks

Size J/10 (6mm), I/9 (5.5mm), H/8 (5mm), G/7 (4.5mm), G/6 (4mm), and F/5 (3.75mm) crochet hooks OR SIZE NEEDED TO OBTAIN GAUGE

Additional

Tapestry needle

Finished Measurements

Finished size 32"/81cm in diameter at bottom hem, 21"/53cm at top hem, and 20"/51cm tall

Gauge

16 sts/2 pattern reps and 8 rows to 4"/10cm over stitch pattern with I/9 (5.5mm) hook.
TAKE TIME TO CHECK YOUR GAUGE.

Note

Ch-3 counts as 1 dc throughout.
Ch-4 counts as 1 dc + 1 ch throughout.

Special Stitches

Picot Ch 3, sl st in 3rd ch from hook.

Cowl

With hook size J/10 (5.5mm) ch 120, join into ring with sl st in first ch, being careful not to twist chain.
Rnd 1 (RS) Ch 1, sc in back or bump of same ch as sl st and in back or bump of each ch around. Join rnd with sl st in first sc—120 sc.
Rnd 2 Ch 1, sc in same sc as sl st, *ch 4, sk 4 sc, sc in next sc; rep from * around until 4 sc remain, ch 4, sk 4 sc, sl st in first sc.
Rnd 3 (RS) Sl st in next ch-4 sp, ch 3, 3 dc in same ch-4 sp, *ch 1, sk 1 sc, 4 dc in next ch-4 sp; rep from * around, ch 1, join rnd with sl st in top of beg-ch. Ch 1, turn.
Rnd 4 (WS) Sc in next ch-1 sp, *ch 4, sk 4 dc, sc in next ch-1 sp; rep from * around until 4 dc remain, ch 4, sk 4 dc, join rnd with sl st in first sc. Turn.
Rep Rnds 3 & 4 three more times. Change to hook size I/9 (5.5mm).
Continue repeating Rnds 3 & 4 for pattern, stepping down one hook size after every 8 rnds until 49 rnds total have been completed; do not turn after Rnd 49.
Rnd 50 Ch 1, sc in first sc, 4 sc in next ch-4 sp, *sc in next sc, 4 sc in next ch-4 sp; rep from * around, join rnd with sl st in first sc—120 sc.
Rnd 51 Ch 1, sc in first sc, *picot, sc in each of next 2 sc; rep from * around, join rnd with sl st in first sc. End off.

Finishing

With hook size J/10 (6mm), rep Rnd 51 on neck opening, working in opposite side of foundation ch. End off. Weave in all ends.

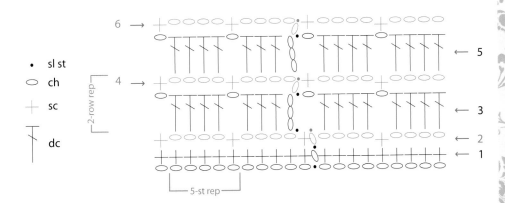

- • sl st
- ◦ ch
- + sc
- ⊤ dc

lime rickey

Yarn ❶
Serenity Sock Solids by Premier Yarns, 1¾oz/50g skeins, each approx 230yd/210m (merino/bamboo/nylon)
- 4 skeins each in Hot Lime #5008

Hook
Size G/6 (4mm) hook OR SIZE NEEDED TO OBTAIN GAUGE

Additional
Tapestry needle

Finished Measurements
26"/66cm tall x 52"/132cm in diameter after blocking

Gauge
6 ch-5 sps and 10 rows to 4"/10cm over pattern st.
TAKE TIME TO CHECK YOUR GAUGE.

Special Stitches
Shell (dc, ch 2, dc) in designated st.

Cowl
Ch 122.
Row 1 Sc in 2nd ch from hook, *ch 5, sk 3 ch, sc in next ch; rep from * to end—30 ch-5 sps. Ch 5, turn.
Row 2 Sc in first ch-5 sp, (ch 5, sc in next ch-5 sp) twice, ch 1, shell in next sc, ch 1, sc in next ch-5 sp, *(ch 5, sc in next ch-5 sp) 3 times, ch 1, shell in next sc, ch 1, sc in next ch-5 sp; rep from * across, (ch 5, sc in next ch-5 sp) twice, ch 2, dc in last sc—7 shells, 23 ch-5 sps. Ch 1, turn.
Row 3 Sc in first dc, (ch 5, sc in next ch-5 sp) twice, *ch 1, shell in next sc, ch 1, sc in next ch-2 sp, ch 1, shell in next sc, ch 1, sc in next ch-5 sp, (ch 5, sc in next ch-5 sp) twice; rep from * across, placing last sc in sp created by t-ch—14 shells, 16 ch-5 sps. Ch 5, turn.
Row 4 Sc in first ch-5 sp, ch 5, sc in next ch-5 sp, ch 5, sc in next ch-2 sp, ch 1, shell in next sc, ch 1, sc in next ch-2 sp, *(ch 5, sc in next ch-5 sp) twice, ch 5, sc in next ch-2 sp, ch 1,

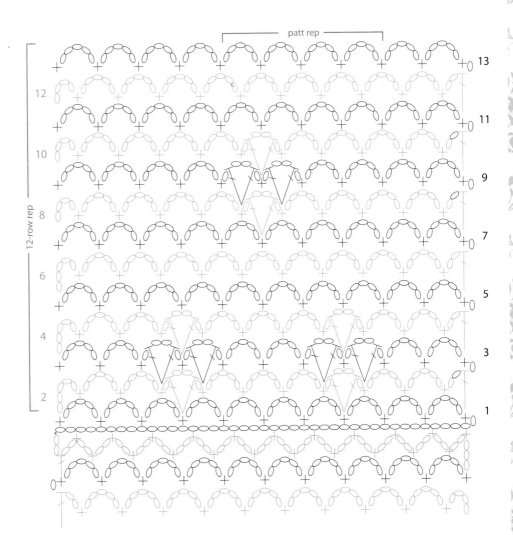

SYMBOL KEY

⬯	ch
+	sc
⊤	dc

lime rickey

shell in next sc, ch 1, sc in next ch-2 sp; rep from * across, (ch 5, sc in next ch-5 sp) twice, ch 2, dc in last sc—7 shells, 23 ch-5 sps. Ch 1, turn.

Row 5 Sc in first dc, (ch 5, sc in next ch-5 sp) twice, *ch 5, sc in next ch-2 sp, (ch 5, sc in next ch-5 sp) 3 times; rep from * to end, placing last sc in sp created by t-ch. Ch 5, turn.

Row 6 Sc in first ch-5 sp, *ch 5, sc in next ch-5 sp; rep from * across, ch 2, dc in last sc. Ch 1, turn.

Row 7 Sc in first dc, *ch 5, sc in next ch-5 sp; rep from * to end, placing last sc in ch-5 sp created by t-ch. Ch 5, turn.

Row 8 Sc in first ch-5 sp, (ch 5, sc in next ch-5 sp) 4 times, ch 1, shell in next sc, ch 1, sc in next ch-5 sp, *(ch 5, sc in next ch-5 sp) 3 times, ch 1, shell in next sc, ch 1 sc in next ch-5 sp; rep from * across, (ch 5, sc in next ch-5 sp) 4 times, ch 2, dc in last sc. Ch 1, turn.

Row 9 Sc in first dc, (ch 5, sc in next ch-5 sp) 4 times, *ch 1, shell in next sc, ch 1, sc in next ch-2 sp, ch 1, shell in next sc, (ch 5, sc in next ch-5 sp) twice; rep from * across, (ch 5, sc in next ch-5 sp) twice more, placing last sc in sp created by t-ch. Ch 5, turn.

Row 10 Sc in first ch-5 sp, (ch 5, sc in next ch-5 sp) 3 times, ch 5, sc in next ch-2 sp, ch 1, shell in next sc, ch 1, sc in next ch-2 sp, *(ch 5, sc in next ch-5 sp) twice, ch 5, sc in next ch-2 sp, ch 1, shell in next sc, ch 1 sc in next ch-2 sp; rep from * across, (ch 5, sc in next ch-5 sp) 4 times, ch 2, dc in last sc. Ch 1, turn.

Row 11 Sc in first dc, (ch 5, sc in next ch-5 sp) 4 times, *ch 5, sc in next ch-2 sp, (ch 5, sc in next ch-5 sp) 3 times; rep from * across, ch 5, sc in sp created by t-ch. Ch 5, turn.

Row 12 Rep Row 6.

Row 13 Rep Row 7.

Rep Rows 2–13 for pattern 8 more times. Do not end off.
Optional: Block piece now—it is easier to make something dry flat than in a moebius shape.

Finishing

Joining

Lay piece flat, lift corners of foundation chain end and flip 180 degrees and lay corners close to other end.

Next Row Ch 3, sc into opposite side of first ch of foundation chain, ch 2, sc in first ch-5 sp of last row, ch 2, sc in first ch-3 sp of foundation ch, *ch 2, sc in next ch-5 sp of last row, ch 2, sc in next ch-3 sp of foundation ch; rep from * across, ch 2, dc in last sc of last row, ch 2, sl st to last ch of foundation ch. Do not end off.

Edging

Rotate work so edge of piece is ready to work.

Rnd 1 Ch 1, 2 sc in sp formed by foundation chain and first ch-5 sp, [work 162 sc evenly across edge as follows: (2 sc in ch-sp formed by t-ch, 1 sc in sp formed by sc) rep to other side of seam], 2 sc in sp before seam, 2 sc in sp after seam, rep bracketed instructions; 2 sc in sp before seam, sl st in first ch to join—328 sc.

Rnd 2 Ch 1, 1 sc in same st as join, ch 6, sk 3 sc, *sc in next sc, ch 6, sk 3 sc; rep from * around, sl st to first ch to join—82 ch-6 sps.

Rnd 3 Ch 1, *[3 sc, (ch 5, sl st in side of last sc made) 3 times, 2 sc] in ch-6 sp; rep from * around, sl st to first ch to join. Fasten off.

Weave in all ends. Block if you haven't done so yet.

strawberry shortcake

Yarn

Stardust by Red Heart, 1¾oz/50g skeins, each approx 191yd/175m (wool/nylon/metallic)
• 3 skeins in Coral #1253

Hooks

Size I/9 (5.5mm), H/8 (5mm), G/7 (4.5mm), G/6 (4mm), and F/5 (3.75mm) crochet hooks

Finished Measurements

23"/58cm tall x 42"/107cm at bottom hem, 30"/76cm at top hem

Gauge

1 motif repeat to 3½"/8.5cm and 8 rows to 4"/10cm over pattern st with largest hook. GAUGE IS NOT CRITICAL FOR THIS PROJECT.

Note

Ch-3 counts as 1 dc throughout.

Cowl

With size I/9 (5.5mm) hook, ch 169. Join into a ring with sl st in first ch, being careful not to twist ch.

Rnd 1 Ch 3, dc in next ch, ch 1, sk 1 ch, dc in next ch, *sk 3 ch, (3 dc, ch 2, 3 dc) in next ch, sk 3 ch, dc in next ch, ch 1, sk 1 ch, dc in each of next 2 ch, ch 1, sk 1 ch, dc in next ch; rep from * around until 9 ch remain, sk 3 ch, (3 dc, ch 2, 3 dc) in next ch, sk 3 ch, dc in next ch, ch 1, join rnd with sl st in top of beg-ch—13 shells.

Rnd 2 Ch 3, dc in next dc, ch 1, dc in next dc, *ch 3, (sc, ch 3, sc) in next ch-2 sp, ch 3, sk 3 dc, dc in next dc, ch 1, dc in

each of next 2 dc, ch 1, dc in next dc; rep from * around, 3 ch, (sc, ch 3, sc) in next ch-2 sp, ch 3, sk 3 dc, dc in next dc, ch 1, join rnd with sl st in top of beg-ch.

Rnd 3 Ch 3, dc in next dc, ch 1, dc in next dc, * sk 3 ch, (3 dc, ch 2, 3 dc) in next ch-3 sp, sk 3 dc, dc in next dc, ch 1, dc in each of next 2 dc, ch 1, dc in next dc; rep from * around, sk ch-3 sp, (3 dc, ch 2, 3 dc) in next ch-3 sp, sk 3 dc, dc in next dc, ch 1, join rnd with sl st in top of beg-ch.

Rep Rnds 2 & 3 for pattern, going down one hook size after every 8 rnds. End off after 7th rnd with smallest hook (a Rnd 2).

Finishing

Top Edging

With smallest hook, with RS facing, join yarn with a sl st in ch-3 sp of any (sc, ch 3, sc).

Rnd 1 Ch 3, (2 dc, ch 2, 3dc) in same ch-3 sp, (3 dc, ch 2, 3 dc) between 2nd and 3rd dc from hook, *sk ch-3 sp, (3 dc, ch 2, 3 dc) in next ch-3 sp, (3 dc, ch 2, 3 dc) between 2nd and 3rd dc from hook; rep from * around, join rnd with sl st in top of beg-ch. End off.

Bottom Edging

With size I/9 (5.5mm) hook, with RS facing, attach yarn in opposite side of foundation ch in base of any 6-dc shell.

Rnd 1 Ch 3, (2 dc, ch 2, 3dc) in same sp, (3 dc, ch 2, 3 dc) between 2nd and 3rd dc from hook, *sk ch-3 sp, (3 dc, ch 2, 3 dc) in base of next 6-dc shell, (3 dc, ch 2, 3 dc) between 2nd and 3rd dc from hook; rep from * around, join rnd with sl st in top of beg-ch. End off.

Weave in all ends. Block lightly if desired.

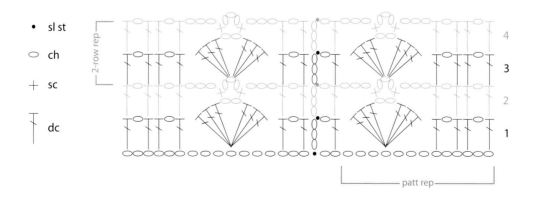

- • sl st
- ◯ ch
- + sc
- ⊤ dc

my notes